UPPER WATERTON LAKE

Waterton Lakes National Park

Located 264 km (165 mi) south of Calgary, Waterton Lakes National Park, Canada's fourth oldest national park, is composed of 525 sq km (203 sq mi) and is home to more than 1,000 varieties of plants, 25 major species of trees, 264 species of birds, almost 60 species of mammals, and 17 species of fish. The park was established in 1895 and originally consisted of only 34.5 sq km (13.5 sq mi). In 1932 Waterton Lakes National Park, Canada, and the adjacent Glacier National Park, USA, became the world's first International Peace Park in recognition of the friendship between these two countries. In 1995 the Waterton/Glacier International Peace Park was designated as a World Heritage Site by UNESCO.

The Waterton Lakes were named by Lt. Thomas Blakiston (1832-1891), a member of the Palliser Expedition, after Charles Waterton (1782-1865), a well-known British naturalist of the 18th century. There are three lakes, Upper Waterton, Middle Waterton and Lower Waterton Lakes. Upper Waterton Lake with an elevation of 1,279 m (4,220 ft) is the largest with a length of 11 km (6.9 mi) and a width of .8 km (.5 mi). With a depth of 148 m (487 ft) the lake is also the deepest lake in the Canadian Rockies. The peaks seen in this photograph from left to right are: Vimy Peak, elevation 2,379 m (7,850 ft), named after the battle of Vimy Ridge in 1917 and Mount Boswell with an elevation of 2,439 m (8,050 ft).

CAMERON LAKE

Waterton Lakes National Park

Located 16 km (10 mi) south of the Waterton townsite at the end of the Akamina Parkway lies beautiful Cameron Lake. Resting in a bowl-shaped cirque formed by glaciers, it lies on the Border Ranges of the Canadian Rocky Mountains and is situated in the subalpine zone at an elevation of 1,660 m (5,480 ft). The combination of elevation and the very moist Pacific winds result in heavy snowfalls at the lake and in the nearby mountains. The average annual precipitation is 42 cm (17 in) of rain and 591 cm (236 in) of snow. It is not unusual for snow to be present for eight months of the year.

Cameron Lake was named by Major General George Mercer Dawson (1849-1901), geologist and Director of the Geological Survey of Canada, in honour of Captain Donald Roderick Cameron (1834-1921), the Canadian Commissioner of the International Boundary Survey of 1872 to 1876. This pristine mountain lake occupies a total area of 172 hectares (425 acres) and is 2.5 km (1.5 mi) in length and .5 km (.3 mi) in width with a depth of 39 metres (129 ft). Pictured in the photograph is Mount Custer in the state of Montana, USA, elevation 2,708 metres (8,936 ft), named after Henry Custer, a topographer with the US Northwestern Boundary Survey of 1861.

THE THREE SISTERS

Kananaskis Country

In 1883 these prominent peaks were known as "The Three Nuns" and provided the backdrop for the small mining community of Canmore, seven kilometres (4.3 mi) to the north, nestled in the Bow Valley. George Mercer Dawson (1849-1901), Director of the Geographical Survey of Canada, renamed this magnificent mountain "The Three Sisters" out of respect for Reverend Robert Terrill Rundle (1811-1896), a Methodist missionary to the Indians of the area during the 1840's, as this was a more appropriate Protestant designation. Story has it that each peak carried the name of one of Reverend Rundle's three sisters. Unofficially the peaks are locally known as Faith, Hope and Charity.

The former Canadian Pacific Railway employees who discovered the hot springs in Banff in 1883, Frank McCabe and the two McCardell brothers, William and Tom, found a coal seam while prospecting just west of the Three Sisters in 1884. In 1886 HRH Queen Victoria (1819-1901) granted a charter to allow coal mining in Canmore. The "Number One Mine" was opened in 1887. It proved to be the best-producing mine of those that were worked in the Bow Valley and remained in operation until its closure in 1979. In 1921, M.B. Morrow, General Manager of the Canmore Coal Company, made the first official ascent of the peaks, climbing the middle Sister at 2,769 metres (9,085 ft).

MOUNT ASSINIBOINE

Mount Assiniboine Provincial Park

Long before the arrival of the explorers and fur traders, the Assiniboine Indians ventured far into the mountains to hunt on the plateau beneath this towering pyramid. Mount Assiniboine was named in their honour by George Mercer Dawson (1849-1901), geologist and Director of the Geological Survey of Canada. Dawson was conducting a topographical survey of the Canadian Rocky Mountains from 1881 to 1884 when he came across this spectacular peak. Sir James Outram (1864-1925), a British alpinist who emigrated to Victoria, British Columbia, in 1900, made the first official ascent of Mount Assiniboine in 1901.

Also known as the "Matterhorn of the Rockies", this prominent peak is located on the border of Banff National Park and Mount Assiniboine Provincial Park in British Columbia, which was established on February 6, 1922 at the urging of the Alpine Club of Canada. The park is only accessible by helicopter or on foot with the shortest and most direct route 27 kilometres (17 mi) in length via the Mount Shark and Bryant Creek trails to Assiniboine Pass. Mount Assiniboine, surrounded by Mount Magog, Lunette Peak, Mount Sturdee and The Marshall, each exceeding 3,100 metres (10,000 ft), is the highest peak in the southern Canadian Rockies standing at an elevation of 3,618 metres (11,870 ft).

MOUNT RUNDLE

Banff National Park

"At 22 kilometres (14 mi) in length, with the Banff townsite at its base, Mount Rundle is perhaps the most recognized landmark in the Canadian Rockies. The 2,949 metre (9,675 ft) peak was named after Robert Terrill Rundle (1811-1896), a Methodist missionary who ministered to the Indians of the region during the 1840's. Sir James Hector (1834-1907) named the mountain in honour of Reverend Rundle in 1858. Hector was the surgeon and geologist of the Palliser Expedition (1857-1860), led by John Palliser (1807-1887), which explored and surveyed much of western British North America.

Robert Terrill Rundle came to Banff from his native England in 1840 as a guest of the Canadian Pacific Railway. He was the first missionary to the Indians of the area and was very highly regarded by them. Rundle learned to speak and write fluently in Cree, the language of the Stoneys. He held many open-air services for them in the meadows at the foot of the mountain which now bears his name and on the shore of Lake Minnewanka. Reverend Rundle lived among the Stoney Indians for eight years while he ministered to them but was forced to return to England due to ill health in 1848.

CASTLE MOUNTAIN

Banff National Park

"Sir James Hector (1834-1907), surgeon and geologist of the Palliser Expedition (1857-1860), first sighted this impressive mountain in 1858. Noting its distinctive appearance he appropriately christened it Castle Mountain. The name stood until 1946 when it was changed to Mount Eisenhower by Canadian Prime Minister William Lyon Mackenzie King (1874-1950) in honour of General Dwight D. Eisenhower (1890-1969), Supreme Commander of the Allied Forces in World War II. In 1979 "Castle Mountain" was officially reinstated, as both Canadians and Americans resented the replacing of such an appropriate and long-standing title. However, the southeast tower of this mountain still bears Eisenhower's name.

Located 30 kilometres (19 mi) northwest of the Banff townsite and standing at an elevation of 2,766 metres (9,075 ft), Castle Mountain is an excellent example of a "castellate" peak. These mountains are common throughout the main ranges, which rise approximately 500 metres (1,640 ft) higher than the peaks of the front ranges. Castellate mountains are similar to "fault thrust" mountains like Mount Rundle, except that the underlying soft layers of shale on the smooth sloped side were eroded away, in this case by the Bow River. This erosion caused the top harder layers of limestone and dolomite to break off, leaving the sheer precipices of today.

LAKE LOUISE

Banff National Park

Lake Louise, known to the Stoney Indians as "The Lake of the Little Fishes", was first visited by guide and outfitter Tom Wilson (1859-1933) and an Indian guide, Edwin Hunter, in 1882. Wilson named it "Emerald Lake" and so it was known until it was renamed by the Canadian Pacific Railway (CPR) after Queen Victoria's fourth daughter, Princess Louise Caroline Alberta (1848-1939). Princess Louise was married to the Marquis of Lorne, Governor General of Canada from 1878 to 1883. Neither Princess Louise nor Queen Victoria ever visited the lake. In the 1890's Lake Louise became a major destination for mountaineers from America, England and Europe.

The peaks seen in this photograph from left to right are: Mount Lefroy, elevation 3,423 metres (11,230 ft), named after Captain John Henry Lefroy (1817-1890), Director of the Magnetic Survey of Canada. Mount Victoria, elevation 3,464 metres (11,365 ft) and the Victoria Glacier, named in honour of HRH Queen Victoria (1819-1901). Mount Whyte, elevation 2,983 metres (9,787 ft), named for Sir William Whyte (1843-1914), Vice-President of the CPR. The Beehive, elevation 2,274 metres (7,460 ft), so named due to its shape by Samuel Evans Stokes Allen (1874-1945). Mount Niblock, elevation 2,976 metres (9,764 ft) named after John Niblock (1849-1914), Western Superintendent of the CPR.

MORAINE LAKE

Banff National Park

Moraine Lake, located 16 kilometres (10 mi) south of the village of Lake Louise, was named by Walter Dwight Wilcox (1869-1949), a Yale graduate who came to the area in 1893 with four of his classmates to explore, map, photograph and survey this newly accessible wilderness. Returning to Lake Louise almost every year of his life thereafter, he found Moraine Lake in 1899 while exploring the valley with Yale colleague, Samuel Evans Stokes Allen (1874-1945). Wilcox thought the lake was formed by blockage from a glacial moraine and so it was named. He published two books popularizing the area which significantly increased the flood of tourists and adventurers.

The valley enclosing the lake is known as the Valley of the Ten Peaks, or the Wenkchemna Peaks. Allen, a linguistic scholar, named them using the Stoney Indian words for the numbers one through ten, "Wenkchemna" meaning ten. Three peaks still retain their original Stoney names but the others were renamed. Peak six was renamed Mount Allen in 1898 by Wilcox. Allen suffered from severe depression brought about by his parents' strong disapproval of his active interest in the Canadian Rockies. After several further trips to the mountains with Wilcox, Samuel Allen was committed to a psychiatric hospital in 1905 where he spent the rest of his life.

PEYTO LAKE

Banff National Park

This magnificent lake fed by the Peyto Glacier, part of the Wapta Icefield, is located 40 kilometres (25 mi) north of Lake Louise on the Icefields Parkway. The lake was named after English born Ebenezer William Peyto (1868-1943) by American writer and explorer Walter Dwight Wilcox (1869-1949). Wilcox greatly admired "Wild" Bill as a guide, outfitter and mountain man and after having travelled hundreds of miles together, considered Peyto to be the best in the Rockies. Peyto was the guide for many famous people of the day including Edward Whymper (1840-1910), the British mountaineer who was the first to conquer the Matterhorn in 1865.

After serving in the Boer War (1899-1902), "Wild" Bill came west to work for the Canadian Pacific Railway and stayed on to become a trapper, prospector, guide and outfitter, specializing in taking adventurous tourists into the wilds of the Canadian Rocky Mountains on horseback. Peyto was known for his dependability, honesty, knowledge of the area and his eccentricity. Always wearing a white scarf, fringed buckskin jacket, wide-brimmed sombrero and well-worn pants he was without question the most colourful figure in Banff. In 1911 Peyto became a warden with the Rocky Mountains Park later known as Banff National Park and headquartered at Healy Creek until his retirement in 1936.

MOUNT ANDROMEDA

Jasper National Park

Located 129 kilometres (80 mi) north of Lake Louise on the Icefields Parkway and standing at an elevation of 3,450 metres (11,319 ft), Mount Andromeda cradles a portion of the massive Columbia Icefield and towers over the giant Athabasca Glacier which slowly flows past its base. This magnificent three peaked summit was named in 1938 by Major Edwin Rex Gibson (1892-1957), Past-President of the Alpine Club of Canada, after the wife of the Greek mythological character, Perseus. Although Mount Andromeda is situated next to the Columbia Icefield, the enormous cirque glacier on the mountain is self-sustaining.

The elevation and the location of the glacier on the north face of Andromeda prevent the snow from melting or evaporating, maintaining the glacier. Average annual snowfall at this elevation is seven to ten metres (23 to 33 ft). Successive snowfalls compress the previous layers into ice granules which in turn are further compressed into a solid layer of ice. The tremendous weight of this ice carves out the rock beneath it into a bowl or cirque. The weight of the glacier and the pull of gravity from below cause the ice to flow over the edge of the cirque down the mountainside. When warm air and sunlight overcome the flow rate of the ice, the glacier stops advancing.

ATHABASCA GLACIER

Jasper National Park

In 1898 two mountain climbers from England, John Norman Collie (1859-1942) and Herman Woolley (1846-1920), made the first official ascent of Mount Athabasca. From the 3,491 metre (11,453 ft) summit, Collie and Woolley discovered the Columbia Icefield, the largest of seventeen named icefields located along the Continental Divide. Covering an area of 325 square kilometres (125 sq mi), the Columbia Icefield is the largest permanent body of ice and snow south of the Arctic Circle and is also the hydrographic apex of North America. Meltwater from the Icefield drains into the Pacific, Arctic and Atlantic Oceans.

The Athabasca Glacier is one of eight large glaciers fed by the Columbia Icefield. Located 95 kilometres (59 mi) south of Jasper and reaching to within one kilometre (.5 mi) of Highway 93, the Athabasca is the most accessible glacier along the Icefields Parkway. Flowing over a series of icefalls below the Columbia Icefield, the massive Athabasca Glacier extends six kilometres (3.75 mi) in length and one kilometre (.5 mi) in width and consists of solid ice that is over 300 metres (1,000 ft) thick. Currently the Athabasca Glacier is receding but other glaciers in the area like the Saskatchewan Glacier are advancing.

MOUNT EDITH CAVELL

Jasper National Park

Located just 29 kilometres (18 mi) south of the Jasper townsite and standing 3,365 metres (11,040 ft) in elevation, Mount Edith Cavell was named to honour the daughter of Anglican minister Reverend John Cavell of Norwich, England. Edith Louisa Cavell (1865-1915) was a nurse and the Matron of the Surgical Institute of Brussels. During the outbreak of the First World War, she tended many Allied soldiers as well as German wounded. As Brussels fell to the advancing Germans, this "angel of mercy" refused to leave her post, choosing instead to continue to care for those in her charge.

On August 15, 1915, Nurse Edith Cavell was arrested by the Germans and charged with assisting English, Belgian and French soldiers to escape and return to their divisions. She was tried and blatantly admitted to the charges. At 2:00 a.m. on October 12, 1915 she was executed, despite attempts to obtain mitigation of her sentence by American Ambassador Bradley Whitlock. Edith Cavell became an inspiration and symbol of courage and dedication to the British people. A memorial service is held annually on the Sunday nearest the date of her arrest at the Anglican Church of St. Mary's and St. George in the town of Jasper.

PYRAMID MOUNTAIN

Jasper National Park

Pyramid Mountain was known as "Priest's Rock" in honour of Father Pierre Jean de Smet (1801-1873) until 1859, when Sir James Hector (1834-1907), surgeon and geologist for the Palliser Expedition (1857-1860), renamed it while on an expedition to the Athabasca Pass. Its resemblance to a pyramid was noted by English adventurer Dr. Walter Butler Cheadle (1835-1910), who travelled across Canada during 1862 and 1863. Lying beneath Pyramid Mountain is Patricia Lake, named in 1914 after Princess Patricia (1886-1974), the daughter of Arthur William Patrick Albert, the Duke of Connaught and Governor General of Canada from 1911 to 1916.

Standing at an elevation of 2,766 metres (9,075 ft) and located only nine kilometres (5.5 mi) northwest of the Jasper townsite, Pyramid Mountain is one of the most prominent landmarks in the area. The mountain consists of Gog quartzite sandstone, first studied near Gog Lake in Mount Assiniboine Provincial Park in British Columbia. Gog quartzite sandstone occurs in thick layers and is unique to the Rocky Mountains due to its hardness, as other sandstone is soft, porous and grainy when broken. The red and orange colour of the rock is caused from iron oxide found in the quartzite.

MALIGNE LAKE

Jasper National Park

To the Stoney Indians it was known as "Chaba Imne", Beaver Lake. In 1908, using a map drawn by a Stoney Indian named Samson Beaver, Mary Schäffer (1861-1939), member of the Academy of Natural Sciences of Philadelphia and of the Geographical Society of America, along with teacher and geologist Mollie Adams, botanist Stewardson Brown, camp cook Reggie Holmes and their two guides Sidney Unwin and Billy Warren, found Maligne Lake. Exploring the lake on a raft which the men had built for the occasion, the group named the surrounding peaks and features, Mounts Unwin, Warren, Mary Vaux, Samson Peak and Samson Narrows.

The term maligne is French for "wicked" and was used by Father Pierre Jean de Smet (1801-1873), a Belgian Jesuit missionary, to describe the treacherous river that flows from the lake. The name soon spread to the lake, canyon, pass, mountain and range. At 22 kilometres (14 mi) in length it is the largest totally glacier-fed lake in North America. Spirit Island at the Samson Narrows is one of the most magnificent scenes in the Canadian Rockies and has kindled the spirit of artists, photographers and writers from around the globe. The pristine waters of Maligne Lake are located 48 kilometres (29 mi) southeast of the town of Jasper.

MOUNT ROBSON

Mount Robson Provincial Park

To the Indians it was known as "Yuh-Lai-Has-Kun", the Mountain of the Spiral Road. There are no official records on file as to whom Mount Robson was named for. However as early as 1863 the mountain was known as "Robson's Peak", probably corrupted from "Robertson". Colin Robertson (1783-1842) was an official with the Hudson's Bay Company in the 1820's and later became a member of Parliament. While with the Hudson's Bay Company, Robertson sent Iroquois fur hunters and trappers into the area. The mountain may have been named to honour John Robson, the Premier of British Columbia from 1889 to 1892, although its name preceded his term in office.

The "Monarch of the Canadian Rockies", standing at 3,954 metres (12,972 ft) in elevation, is the highest peak in the Canadian Rocky Mountains. Located 85 kilometres (54 mi) west of the Jasper townsite, it towers over the western entrance to Mount Robson Provincial Park, established as British Columbia's second provincial park on March 1, 1913. On July 31 of the same year, Conrad Kain (1883-1934), Albert Henry MacCarthy (1876-1955) and Col. William Washborough Foster (1875-1954) made the first official ascent of Mount Robson. They climbed the northeast face, now known as the Kain Face and descended by the south face to Kinney Lake.

Published with pride in Alberta, Canada by

Bela Baliko Photography and Publishing Inc.
158 Benchlands Terrace
Canmore, Alberta, Canada   T1W 1G2
Telephone/Fax: (403) 678-2010
e-mail: bbaliko@teluspla.net

Editing, Layout and Design: Bela Baliko
Research and Editing: Susan Louise Baliko
Printed in Calgary, Alberta by Ronalds Printing
Printed using Environmentally Friendly Materials

ISBN 0-921146-90-6